LUSCIOUS CREAMY DESSERTS

IMP Limited

CONTENTS

CHOOSING CREAM

Cream adds a wonderful flourish to any dessert, from a simple bowl of berries to a rich cheesecake. Here is a guide to choosing the best cream to accompany your dish.

CREAM FOR WHIPPING

Double and whipping creams are suitable for whipping. To whip, simply beat air into the cream, using a hand-held or an electric whisk (a hand-held whisk gives more control over the texture).

For the best results, chill the bowl, whisk and cream before whipping. It is a lot easier to whip cream in a bowl that is only half full — too much cream makes it difficult to beat in enough air and the cream will take longer to whip. Take care not to overwhip or the cream will separate into butter granules and buttermilk.

Fully whipped cream should stand in soft peaks, stick to the whisk and keep its shape. Whipped cream is best used immediately, but if you chill it in the fridge, it will hold its shape for about 3–4 hours.

CREAM FOR PIPING

Double and whipping creams are best for piping, but don't whip the cream too stiffly as it will thicken when forced through the piping bag nozzle. Whip double cream until it is one and a half times its original volume and whipping cream until it has doubled in volume.

CREAM FOR FREEZING

• Double and whipping creams keep in the freezer for two months, if half-whipped first.
• Freeze clotted cream in its container for one month. Thaw in the fridge before using.
• Single, sour and half-cream are not suitable for freezing.
• Pipe whipped cream into rosettes and open-freeze until firm; pack in a rigid container with freezer wrap between layers. Use from frozen.
• Cream can be bought ready frozen in stick or chip form.

BLENDED CREAM

These buttermilk and vegetable oil blends are a long-lasting alternative to cream.

4

...pping cream (...ht) has a fat ...tent of 35% ... is ...ellent for ...ng. It can ...kept, ...pened, ...he fridge ... 14 days.

Sour cream (right) has a sharp taste created by adding a natural culture. With a fat content of 18%, it can't be whipped. It will keep, unopened, in the fridge for 7–10 days.

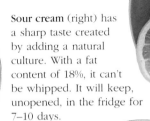

Extra thick double cream (left) is ideal for spooning onto fruit and puddings. It has a fat content of 48% and will not freeze. It can be kept, unopened, in the fridge for up to 14 days.

Clotted cream (left) is rich, golden and very thick — perfect for spreading. With a high fat content of 55%, it is not ideal for cooking, as it separates easily. It can be kept in the fridge, unopened, for 14 days.

Single cream (left) has a fat content of 18% and is perfect for pouring, but too thin for whipping. It can only be frozen once combined with other ingredients. It can be kept, unopened, in the fridge for 14 days.

Double cream (left) is ideal for pouring, whipping and piping. It has a fat content of 48%. It freezes well, so it is ideal for making ice cream and can also be boiled. It will keep, unopened, in the fridge for 14 days.

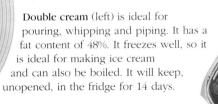

SERVING TIP Sponge finger biscuits make a good accompaniment to this tangy dessert. Or serve brandy snaps or shortbread fingers, as their 'crunch' contrasts deliciously with the fluffy mousse.

LEMON AND LIME MOUSSE

SOUTHERN ITALY

Lemons and limes grow in the warmth of the Mediterranean sun and this light, refreshing mousse has a deliciously citrus tang. A quick, year-round dessert that everyone will love.

INGREDIENTS
(Serves 4)

- 2 sheets leaf gelatine
- 2 limes
- 1 lemon
- 284ml/10fl oz double cream
- 125g/4½oz caster sugar
- 2 egg whites or 1 sachet powdered egg white, reconstituted (see page 62)

TO DECORATE

- 1 lemon
- 1 lime, sliced thinly

INGREDIENTS TIP

Leaf gelatine, available from supermarkets, is easy to use and gives foolproof results. Following the instructions given on the packet, simply soak the sheets in cold water for a few minutes. Squeeze out the excess water. Add the gelatine sheets to the hot liquid used in the recipe and stir briskly until they dissolve.

1 Soak the gelatine in plenty of cold water for 5 minutes to soften it.

2 Wash the limes and lemon under hot water and dry with kitchen paper. Grate the rind finely and squeeze the juice. Mix together the grated rinds, juice and any pulp left over from the squeezed fruit.

3 Heat the juice in a bowl without boiling, then remove from the heat. Squeeze the water out of the gelatine. Dissolve in the warm fruit juice, stirring briskly.

4 In a bowl, whip the cream with the sugar until soft peaks form. Stir in the dissolved gelatine mixture until evenly combined. Cover and chill for 15 minutes or until starting to set.

5 With a clean whisk, beat the egg whites or reconstituted egg white until stiff. Fold into the cream mixture with a balloon whisk or large metal spoon. Divide the mousse between 4 dessert bowls and chill for 1 hour, or until set. To serve, peel thin slices of lemon rind and cut into strips. Use lime slices and lemon strips to decorate mousses.

Step 3

Step 4

Step 5

Preparation **30** Min
Chilling **1** Hour **15** Min
Per Serving: 390 kcal/1622 kJ
4g protein; 30g fat; 29g carbohydrate

TYPICALLY SICILIAN

Sicily grows 90% of Italy's lemon crop and the lemon is just one of the many fruits and vegetables that grow abundantly on this sunny island. Other important crops include peppers, artichokes, aubergines and tomatoes, which all feature in Sicilian dishes.

PANNA COTTA WITH BLACKBERRY SAUCE

SOUTHERN ITALY

Panna Cotta, the Italian for cooked cream, is a smooth vanilla-scented confection that simply melts in the mouth. Here it is served with a dark fruit purée and crunchy nuts.

INGREDIENTS
(Serves 4)

- 500ml/18fl oz whipping cream
- 4 tbsp caster sugar
- 1 vanilla pod
- 2 sheets leaf gelatine
- 250g/9oz blackberries
- 2 tbsp icing sugar
- 1 tbsp Grappa
- 2 tbsp chopped pistachios, to decorate

INGREDIENTS TIP

Grappa is an Italian spirit similar to brandy. It has a strong, fiery flavour and is often added to Italian desserts. Brandy would make a good substitute or, for this recipe, crème de cassis, a French liqueur made from blackcurrants.

1 Put the cream and sugar in a pan. Slit the vanilla pod and scrape the seeds into the pan. Add the split pod and heat gently.

2 Simmer over a low heat for 15–20 minutes, stirring occasionally, until thick. Remove from the heat. Soak the gelatine in plenty of cold water for 5 minutes.

3 Squeeze the water from the gelatine. Put 3 tablespoons of water in a cup and stand in a pan of hot water. Add the gelatine and stir until dissolved. Remove the vanilla pod from the cream and stir in the gelatine.

4 Rinse four 6.5cm/2¾in diameter moulds with cold water and pour in the cream. Cover and chill for about 3 hours until set.

5 Wash the blackberries. Reserve a few for decoration and purée the rest by pushing them through a sieve with a spoon. Stir in the icing sugar and Grappa.

6 Remove the moulds from the fridge 30 minutes before serving. Spoon the purée onto 4 plates. Turn out the creams (see Cooking Tips). Place onto the purée. Decorate with blackberries and pistachios.

Step 1

Step 5

Step 6

Preparation **30** Min Chilling **3** Hours
Per Serving: 675 kcal/2801 kJ;
15g protein; 56g fat; 27g carbohydrate

TYPICALLY ITALIAN

Modern methods of production mean that the wines from southern Italy are gaining ground on their more famous northern counterparts. The sunny climate is particularly suitable for the sweeter dessert wines, Marsala and Moscato, which are favoured in the south.

COOKING TIPS

Rinsing the moulds in cold water and pouring in the mixture without drying the moulds first makes turning out easier. You can also line the base of each mould with greaseproof paper • When the dessert is set, loosen the edge with a palette knife. Invert the mould, slide the cream onto the blade, then transfer to a plate.

SERVING TIP

Serve with flavoured coffee, such as Amaretto or Irish Cream. Instead of the blackberries and pistachios, you could drizzle a caramel sauce over the top of each cream and decorate with fine strips of candied orange peel.

3 WAYS WITH ICE CREAM

*Complement real, home-made vanilla ice cream with coffee,
strawberries or bananas for a deliciously cool, summer delight.*

BASIC VANILLA ICE CREAM

Preparation **30** Min
Freezing **8–9** Hours

(SERVES 4)
- 500ml/18fl oz milk
- 4 egg yolks
- 60g/2½oz caster sugar
- 1 tsp vanilla essence
- 125ml/4fl oz double cream

1 Heat the milk in a pan until hot but not boiling. Whisk the yolks with the sugar until thick and light. Stir in the milk.

2 Return to the pan and heat, stirring constantly, without boiling, until the mixture is thick enough to coat the back of the spoon. Cool; stir in the vanilla.

3 Pour into a shallow freezer container and freeze for 2–3 hours until slushy. Empty into a bowl or blender and beat vigorously to break up the ice crystals.

4 Whip the cream until soft peaks form and fold in. Return to the freezer for 6 hours until firm. Use within 1 month.

ITALIAN COFFEE CUP
Preparation **15** Min

SOUTHERN ITALY

- 1 quantity basic vanilla ice cream
- 200ml/7fl oz very strong black coffee
- 4 tbsp Amaretto (almond liqueur)
- 125ml/4fl oz whipping cream
- 25g/1oz caster sugar
- 2 tbsp toasted flaked almonds
- 2 tbsp drinking chocolate powder

5 Mix the coffee and Amaretto together and cool. Whip the cream to soft peaks and whisk in the sugar.

6 Scoop the ice cream into sundae glasses and pour over the coffee mixture. Spoon the cream into a piping bag fitted with a star nozzle and pipe a swirl on top. Sprinkle each dessert with the flaked almonds and a little drinking chocolate.

BANANA SUNDAE

CARIBBEAN

- 1 quantity basic vanilla ice cream
- 2 ripe bananas
- 3 tbsp lemon juice
- 125ml/4fl oz whipping cream
- 4 tbsp rum
- 4 tbsp chocolate sauce
- ice cream cigar wafers
- 4 tbsp toasted desiccated coconut

5 Peel and slice the bananas and sprinkle them with lemon juice. Whip the cream until it forms soft peaks.

6 Scoop the vanilla ice cream into sundae glasses. Add the banana slices and sprinkle with rum.

7 Spoon the cream into a piping bag fitted with a star nozzle and pipe a swirl of whipped cream on each serving.

8 Pour over the chocolate sauce and serve, decorated with cigar wafers and desiccated coconut.

ICE CREAM ROMANO

RUSSIA

- 1 quantity basic vanilla ice cream
- 500g/1lb strawberries
- 4 tbsp Maraschino liqueur or Kirsch (cherry brandy)
- 4 tbsp brandy

5 At least 30 minutes before serving, put the basic vanilla ice cream in the fridge to soften.

6 Meanwhile, wash the strawberries. Pat dry on kitchen paper. Cut the strawberries in half and divide between 4 serving bowls.

7 Mix together the Maraschino or Kirsch and brandy. Stir the liqueur mixture into the softened vanilla ice cream. Spoon the ice cream over the strawberries and serve at once.

CLASSIC TIRAMISU

NORTHERN ITALY

Rich and unbelievably creamy, this Italian pudding is now an international favourite. Cream cheese, coffee and almond liqueur are its traditional flavourings.

INGREDIENTS
(Serves 6)

- 2 tbsp caster sugar
- 150ml/¼ pint whipping cream
- 250g/9oz mascarpone
- 1 lemon
- 90ml/3fl oz very strong black coffee
- 5 tbsp Amaretto (almond liqueur)
- 225g/8oz sponge fingers

TO DECORATE
- 1 tbsp cocoa powder

INGREDIENTS TIP

Mascarpone is an Italian full-fat, unsalted cream cheese made from cows' milk. As an alternative, 100g/4oz cream cheese stirred into 150ml/¼ pint double cream could be used. Amaretto is available in miniatures. Use two if you are buying it especially for the recipe or replace it with brandy or Tia Maria.

1 Put the sugar, whipping cream and mascarpone into a bowl. Wash the lemon and dry on kitchen paper. Grate the rind and squeeze the juice. Add the lemon rind and juice to the bowl and beat the contents together with an electric whisk or a wooden spoon until thick and creamy.

2 Mix the black coffee with the Amaretto in a small bowl. Dip half the sponge fingers in the coffee mixture, then lay them side by side in the base of a 1.2 litre/2 pint shallow, rectangular dish.

3 Spread half the mascarpone cream mixture over the sponge fingers, making sure that they are covered completely.

4 Dip the remaining sponge fingers in the coffee mixture. Lay them on top of the previous layer and spread with the remaining mascarpone cream. Cover the dish with cling film and chill in the fridge for at least 3 hours.

5 Remove the tiramisù from the fridge about 30 minutes before serving. Sift the cocoa powder over the surface and serve.

Step 1

Step 2

Step 4

Preparation **40** Min Chilling **3** Hours
Per Serving: 350 kcal/1453 kJ
6g protein; 25g fat; 20g carbohydrate

TYPICALLY TUSCAN

Since the last century Tuscany, and in particular Florence, has been a popular holiday destination for the English. Early visitors enjoyed Zuppa Inglese, a dessert similar to trifle that was named in their honour. Tiramisù is a modern version of this.

COOKING TIP

When dipping the sponge fingers in the coffee and Amaretto mixture, leave them immersed in the liquid for about 30 seconds so they absorb as much of it as possible. When all have been dipped, spoon any liquid remaining in the bowl over the sponge fingers already in the dish.

SERVING TIP

A glass of sweet dessert wine such as an Italian Moscato or vin santo could be served with this rich dessert. A creamy cappuccino, sprinkled with a little cocoa powder, would also make a good accompaniment.

CHOCOLATE ORANGE BOMBE

A sumptuous and truly stunning dessert. Chocolate and orange ice creams are hidden beneath an impressive dome of Swiss roll slices filled with chocolate buttercream.

INGREDIENTS
(Serves 12)

- 3 large eggs
- 75g/3oz caster sugar, plus extra to sprinkle
- 60g/2½oz plain flour
- ½ tsp baking powder
- 25g/1oz cocoa powder
- 50g/2oz butter, softened
- 75g/3oz icing sugar
- 50g/2oz candied orange peel
- 600ml/1 pint soft scoop chocolate ice cream
- 2 tbsp orange liqueur
- 425ml/14fl oz soft scoop vanilla ice cream
- strawberries, mint leaves, whipped cream, to decorate

INGREDIENTS TIP

Cocoa powder has a strong flavour and is ideal for flavouring cakes. Substitute a luxury chocolate Swiss roll instead of making your own.

1 Preheat the oven to 200°C/400°F/Gas 6. Line a 30x23cm/12x9in Swiss roll tin with non-stick baking paper. Whisk the eggs and caster sugar together with an electric whisk until very thick and pale in colour.

2 Sift the flour, baking powder and half the cocoa powder and fold into the mixture. Spread out evenly in the tin and bake for 12 minutes. Sprinkle a clean tea towel with caster sugar. Invert sponge onto the towel and peel off the old paper. Fold in one long edge and roll up loosely with the towel inside. Leave to cool and set, then unroll.

3 Blend the remaining cocoa powder with a little water. Cream the butter until soft. Gradually beat in the icing sugar, then the cocoa. Spread over sponge and roll up again.

4 Line a 1.7 litre/3 pint pudding basin with cling film. Cut the sponge into 1cm/½in slices and line the basin with two-thirds of the slices. Chop the candied peel. Spoon the chocolate ice cream into the bowl. Stir the liqueur and candied peel into the vanilla ice cream and spoon on top. Cover with the remaining sponge and freeze for 4 hours. Turn out, remove the cling film and decorate.

Step 2

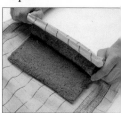

Step 2

Step 4

Preparation **1** Hour **20** Min
Cooking **12** Min Freezing **4** Hours
Per Serving: 359 kcal/1521 kJ;
9g protein; 9g fat; 65g carbohydrate

TYPICALLY TUSCAN

In Tuscany, this recipe is called Zucotto after its resemblance to the famous cathedral dome in Florence. Another popular frozen Italian dessert is Cassata, a bombe with nuts and dried fruits added to vanilla, strawberry and pistachio ice creams.

COOKING TIP

It's the air trapped in the whisked eggs that makes the sponge rise when it is baked, rather than the addition of a raising agent. So it is important to make sure the whisked eggs and dry ingredients are folded in very gently to ensure the air is not knocked out, which would result in a heavy, rubbery sponge.

SERVING TIP

Decorate the dessert with lines of piped whipped cream. In Italy these would be piped in lines, to resemble the cathedral dome in Florence that the dessert imitates.

15

$\mathscr{S}$TRAWBERRY CREAM WHIP

SWITZERLAND

Dreamy layers of fresh strawberries and lightly frozen cream mixed with yoghurt make this a summery dessert. A rosette of whipped cream and crunchy walnuts provide the finishing touch

INGREDIENTS
(Serves 4)

- 500g/1lb 2oz strawberries
- 25g/1oz caster sugar
- ½ tsp vanilla essence
- 1 tbsp icing sugar
- 1 tbsp clear honey

FOR THE WHIP
- 1 small lemon
- 325g/11oz natural yoghurt
- 2 tbsp icing sugar
- 200ml/7fl oz whipping cream

TO DECORATE
- 90ml/3fl oz whipping cream
- 2 tbsp chopped nuts

INGREDIENTS TIP

Strawberries spoil quickly so it is best to use them as soon as possible after buying or picking. If you need to store them, discard any fruit that is bruised or mouldy.

1 Rinse the strawberries in a colander under cold running water and pat dry with kitchen paper. Pull out the stalks, then roughly chop the berries.

2 Whisk together the caster sugar, vanilla essence, icing sugar and honey until smooth. Stir in the strawberries. Cover and chill for 2–3 hours to draw out their juices.

Step 2

3 For the whip, wash the lemon in hot water and dry. Grate the rind finely and squeeze the juice. Mix with the yoghurt and icing sugar. Whip the cream until soft peaks form and fold into the yoghurt mixture. Spoon into a shallow freezer container, cover and freeze for 3–4 hours, or until half frozen.

Step 3

4 Put the whip in a food processor, or blender, and blend briefly. Layer the strawberry mixture and the whip in 4 tall dessert glasses, finishing with the strawberries.

5 Whip the cream until soft peaks form. Spoon it into a piping bag fitted with a star nozzle. Decorate each serving with a rosette of whipped cream and a sprinkling of chopped nuts. Serve immediately.

Step 5

Preparation **45** Min Chilling **2-3** Hours
Freezing **3-4** Hours
Per Serving: 361 kcal/1502 kJ;
6g protein; 24g fat; 33g carbohydrate

TYPICALLY SWISS
The Swiss like to preserve as much of their culture as possible and in some parts of the country, milk churns are still transported by horse and cart. Local specialities using fresh cream, such as cheese tarts and chocolate cakes, can be enjoyed in country inns.

COOKING TIP

Freezing the yoghurt and cream mixture for 3–4 hours allows sufficient time for ice crystals to form, but not long enough for the mixture to become completely solid. The mixture is then puréed in a food processor, or blender, to break up the ice crystals and give the dessert a deliciously thick, granita-like consistency.

SERVING TIP

Round off a celebratory meal with this fruity whip. A medium dry sparkling white wine, such as Asti Spumante, would make a good accompaniment.

SERVING TIP Serve with a small glass of sweet dessert wine such as Marsala, or with a fruit or coffee liqueur such as Cointreau or Baileys poured over cubes of ice.

$\mathscr{S}$WISS CHOCOLATE TRIFLE

SWITZERLAND

A feather-light chocolate sponge is steeped in brandy, sprinkled with fresh redcurrants, then covered with a thick layer of custard and attractively decorated to make this dreamy dessert.

INGREDIENTS

(Serves 8)

- 600ml/1 pint milk
- 50g/2oz granulated sugar
- 50g/2oz custard powder
- 3 small eggs
- 100g/4oz caster sugar
- 40g/1½oz cornflour
- 40g/1½oz plain flour
- 2 tbsp cocoa powder
- 5 tbsp Kirsch or brandy
- 450g/1lb redcurrants
- ½ tsp vanilla essence
- 142ml/5fl oz whipping cream
- 4 thin chocolate squares

INGREDIENTS TIP

Bought trifle sponges can be used instead of home-made sponge. Wafer-thin chocolate squares are available from the confectionery section of larger supermarkets.

1 Make 600ml/1 pint custard using the milk, granulated sugar and custard powder, following the packet instructions. Cover with a sheet of damp greaseproof paper to prevent a skin forming. Cool for 30 minutes.

2 Preheat the oven to 200°C/400°F/Gas 6. Whisk the eggs, half the caster sugar and 2 tablespoons hot water in a bowl for 5 minutes until the whisk leaves a thick trail on the surface. Sift the cornflour, flour and cocoa into the mixture and lightly fold in. Grease a 20cm/8in square cake tin. Spoon in the mixture and cook for 15 minutes, or until a skewer pushed into the centre comes out clean. Remove from the oven and cool.

3 Turn out the sponge and break or cut into bite-sized pieces. Put into a serving bowl and sprinkle with the Kirsch or brandy.

4 Wash the redcurrants and remove from the stalks. Mix with the remaining sugar and vanilla, then spoon on top of the sponge; pour over the custard. Whip the cream until soft peaks form. Spoon into a piping bag fitted with a star nozzle and pipe rosettes over the custard. Cut each chocolate square into two triangles and press into the cream rosettes.

Step 2

Step 3

Step 4

Preparation **50** Min Cooking **15** Min
Per Serving: 276 kcal/1159 kJ
5g protein; 12g fat; 35g carbohydrate

TYPICALLY SWISS

Chocolate is made from cocoa powder, cocoa solids and sugar and was first produced commercially in Switzerland. The country is still famous for making fine chocolate with a superior flavour from the high percentage of cocoa solids it contains.

SERVING TIP Serve these creamy desserts in knickerbocker glory glasses or sundae dishes to reveal the succulent berries inside. Wafer or shortbread biscuits make a crisp accompaniment.

SUMMER FRUIT CUPS

GERMANY

The fresh, tart flavour of rhubarb is the perfect foil for the soft, sweetened cheese mixture and the luscious ripe strawberries that make up these colourful fruit cups.

INGREDIENTS
(Serves 4)

- 500g/1lb 2oz rhubarb
- 150ml/¼ pint orange juice
- 75g/3oz caster sugar
- ½ tsp ground cinnamon
- 1-2 tsp cornflour
- 200g/7oz curd cheese
- 25g/1oz caster sugar
- ½ tsp vanilla essence
- 100ml/3½fl oz whipping cream
- 250g/9oz strawberries

INGREDIENTS TIP

Although, strictly speaking, rhubarb is a vegetable and not a fruit, it is almost always used in sweet recipes. Early forced, spring rhubarb is pink and sweet, while the later maincrop variety has a darker colour and more acidic taste.

1 Wash and dry the rhubarb. Trim away any leaves and peel any stringy fibres from the stalks. Cut into 1–2cm/½–¾in pieces.

2 Put the rhubarb, orange juice, sugar and cinnamon in a pan and bring to the boil. Lower the heat and simmer for 2 minutes until the rhubarb has softened.

3 Mix the cornflour with 1 tablespoon cold water until smooth, add to the pan and bring back to the boil, stirring constantly. Simmer for 1 minute until the juices thicken, then remove from heat and allow to cool.

4 For the cream mixture, mix the curd cheese, sugar and vanilla essence together with a large metal spoon. Whip the cream until soft peaks form and gently fold into the cheese mixture.

5 Wash the strawberries, pat dry with kitchen paper, then reserve 4 for decoration. Remove the stalks and halve the berries. Fold the curd cheese mixture and strawberries into the rhubarb with a spatula. Spoon into 4 tall dessert glasses and chill for 1 hour. To serve, top each dessert with a fresh whole strawberry.

Step 1

Step 2

Step 5

Preparation **20** Min Cooking **5** Min
Chilling **1** Hour
Per Serving: 375 kcal/1571 kJ;
9g protein; 20g fat; 43g carbohydrate

TYPICALLY GERMAN

Rhubarb was introduced to Germany from Britain 200 years ago and has been widely cultivated there ever since. It is in season from April to July, and used in all kinds of fruit cakes and breads or puréed with cream for light desserts.

*V*ANILLA CREAM WITH RASPBERRIES

GERMANY

*This traditional Bavarian dessert is a mix of hot and cold —
cool, creamy base topped with warm raspberry sauce. Not only
to be enjoyed in Germany — it's a treat in any country.*

INGREDIENTS
(Serves 6)

- 3 sheets leaf gelatine
- 1 tsp vanilla essence
- 375ml/12fl oz milk
- 75g/3oz caster sugar
- 142ml/5fl oz whipping
  cream

FOR THE RASPBERRY SAUCE
- 325g/11oz raspberries
- 3 tbsp icing sugar
- 2 tbsp orange liqueur

TO DECORATE
- lemon balm or mint sprigs

INGREDIENTS TIP

The orange liqueur can be
replaced with orange juice
so children as well as adults
can enjoy the dessert.

1 Soak the gelatine in plenty of water for
5 minutes. Meanwhile, stir the vanilla
essence into the milk in a pan, bring to the
boil, then remove from the heat and add in
the sugar, stirring until it dissolves.

2 Squeeze excess water from the gelatine,
add to the hot milk and stir until it has
dissolved. Allow the milk to cool.

Step 1

3 Whip the cream until soft peaks form
and fold it into the milk. Pour the
mixture into a 500ml/18fl oz dessert mould
and chill in the fridge for about 4 hours,
until set.

4 Wash the raspberries and remove any
stalks. Reserve a few berries for
decoration, then press the remainder
through a fine sieve into a pan. Mix in the
icing sugar and orange liqueur. Carefully
heat the sauce until just warmed through.

Step 4

5 To serve, dip the mould into a bowl of
hot water for a few seconds, then turn
the vanilla cream out onto a serving plate.
Drizzle the warmed raspberry sauce over
the top and decorate with the reserved
raspberries and lemon balm or mint leaves.

Step 5

Preparation **50** Min Chilling 4 Hours
Per Serving: 288 kcal/1204 kJ;
4g protein; 20g fat; 23g carbohydrate

TYPICALLY BAVARIAN
This most elegant culinary invention, a
creamy set custard, is internationally known
as a bavarois. Legend has it that the dessert
was created in the 14th century by a chef
who worked for a Bavarian princess, later to
become Queen Isabelle of France.

COOKING TIPS

To turn out the dessert, first loosen the edge from the side of the mould. This enables air to penetrate and release the vacuum around the cream • If you prefer, pour the cream mixture into a serving dish and, when set, spoon it directly onto individual plates and hand the sauce round separately.

SERVING TIP

For a decorative effect, spoon 3-4 tablespoons of pouring cream around the base of the dessert, surround it with raspberry sauce and swirl the two together with a cocktail stick.

ℛICH CHOCOLATE MOUSSE

NORTHERN FRANCE

This heavenly, fluffy treat is a favourite dessert to round off a festive dinner. Its melt-in-the-mouth texture and creamy taste are totally irresistible to chocoholics everywhere.

INGREDIENTS
(Serves 4)

- 50g/2oz softened butter
- 150g/5oz good-quality plain chocolate
- 4 egg whites or 2 sachets powdered egg whites, reconstituted (see page 62)
- 2 tbsp caster sugar

TO DECORATE
- 50g/2oz white chocolate
- mint sprigs

INGREDIENTS TIP
Dark chocolate with a high percentage of cocoa solids should be used for this recipe so that the mousse has a rich, strong flavour. Look for brands of chocolate which have a cocoa solid content of at least 60%.

1 Cut the butter into small pieces and chop or break up the chocolate. Place in a pan and melt slowly over a low heat, stirring occasionally with a wooden spoon.

2 As soon as the chocolate and butter have melted completely, remove from the heat, transfer to a bowl and leave to cool.

Step 1

3 When the chocolate mixture has cooled completely, whisk the egg whites until soft peaks form. Add the sugar and continue whisking until stiff.

4 Gradually fold the whisked egg whites into the chocolate mixture. Spoon the mousse into a pudding basin and chill for at least 3 hours until set.

Step 4

5 Chill the white chocolate, then finely grate it. Remove the mousse from the fridge and use a dessertspoon to scoop out a portion. Place another similar sized spoon on top to shape it into an oval, or egg shape.

6 Use the second spoon to gently slide three scoops of mousse on to each serving plate, then sprinkle with the grated white chocolate. Decorate with a mint sprig.

Step 5

Preparation **25** Min Chilling **3** Hours
Per Serving: 405 kcal/1690 kJ
5g protein; 26g fat; 40g carbohydrate

TYPICALLY FRENCH
Chocolate desserts are very popular in France and are always made with dark, bitter chocolate, never the sweet milk variety favoured in Britain. It is rare to find a restaurant in France without the chef's chocolate mousse à la maison on the menu.

COOKING TIPS

For a real treat, enhance the flavour with a dash of cognac — stir 2 tablespoons into the melted chocolate mixture • Stir 1 tablespoon of the whisked egg white into the chocolate mixture before folding in the rest. This loosens the chocolate mixture and makes it easier to incorporate the egg white evenly.

SERVING TIP

For a contrast of flavours, accompany the chocolate mousse with orange segments drizzled with a little orange liqueur.

CHILLED RASPBERRY SOUFFLES

NORTHERN FRANCE

These individual fruit soufflés make an impressive dinner party dessert. The orange liqueur gives the cool raspberry cream extra richness and flavour.

INGREDIENTS

(Serves 4)

- 2 sheets leaf gelatine
- 1 lemon
- 325g/11oz raspberries
- 4 tbsp caster sugar
- 2 tbsp orange liqueur
- 142ml/5fl oz whipping cream
- 2 egg whites or 1 sachet powdered egg white, reconstituted (see page 62)
- 142ml/5fl oz sour cream

TO DECORATE

- 284ml/10fl oz whipping cream
- 36 raspberries

INGREDIENTS TIP

Frozen raspberries can be used if fresh are not available. Defrost them sufficiently for them to be puréed and transfer those needed for decoration to a plate lined with kitchen paper.

1 Soak the sheets of gelatine in plenty of cold water for 5 minutes. Wash the lemon in hot water and dry. Grate the rind and squeeze the juice into a bowl.

2 Purée the raspberries in a food processor or blender, then push through a sieve. Stir 3 tablespoons of sugar and the lemon rind and juice into the purée.

Step 2

3 Warm 4 tablespoons raspberry purée in a small pan; remove from heat. Squeeze the water out of the gelatine. Add to the pan and stir until dissolved. Stir this mixture and the orange liqueur into the raspberry purée.

4 Whip the whipping cream with the remaining sugar until thick enough to hold its shape. With clean beaters, whisk the egg whites into soft peaks. Fold the sour cream, whipped cream and egg whites into the purée.

Step 4

5 Make a 5cm/2in collar of doubled foil for each of four 9cm/3½in ramekin dishes, and secure with elastic bands. Divide the soufflé between the dishes and chill for 3 hours until firm. Carefully remove the foil and wipe the ramekins clean. Whip the cream; decorate the soufflés with cream rosettes and raspberries.

Step 5

Preparation **50** Min Chilling **3** Hours
Per Serving: 238 kcal/988 kJ;
2g protein; 20g fat; 13g carbohydrate

TYPICALLY FRENCH

Alsace, in France's north-east corner on its border with Germany, is a gourmet's paradise. Its gastronomy combines the richness of German cooking with the subtlety of French cuisine. It is well known for its cherry brandy, which is called Kirsch.

COOKING TIPS

Sieving the raspberry purée removes the tiny
raspberry pips and gives the finished soufflés a
smoother texture • To remove the foil from each
soufflé and create a clean edge, dip a palette knife
in hot water, then slide it around the inside of the
foil collar first.

SERVING TIP

Serve this dessert after a
sophisticated fish dish such
as tuna steak with chilli dressing
and pepper sauce. The smooth but
tangy soufflé will complement the spicy
main course.

CRÈME BRULEE

NORTHERN FRANCE

Here is a velvety smooth dessert of eggs, cream and fragrant vanilla topped with a crusty layer of caramelized sugar. Crack the topping with a spoon to reveal the scrumptious mixture below.

INGREDIENTS
(Serves 6)

- 2 vanilla pods or 1 tsp vanilla essence
- 284ml/10fl oz whipping cream
- pinch of salt
- 2 large egg yolks
- 2 small eggs
- 25g/1oz caster sugar

FOR THE CARAMEL
- 40g/1½oz caster sugar

INGREDIENTS TIP
Although vanilla pods give the purest flavour, vanilla essence makes an acceptable alternative. Buy pure essence, rather than vanilla flavouring, which is extracted from clove oil and gives an artificial, less subtle taste.

1 Preheat the oven to 170°C/325°F/Gas 3. Line a roasting tin with paper, fill with 3cm/1¼in hot water and place in the oven.

2 If using, slit open the vanilla pods lengthways and scrape out the seeds into a pan. Add the pods or essence, cream and salt, bring to the boil. Remove from the heat.

3 Whisk the egg yolks, the whole eggs and caster sugar together in a bowl until light and creamy. Remove the pods, if using, from the cream, then pour the cream gradually into the egg mixture, whisking continuously.

4 Strain through a fine sieve into six 125ml/4fl oz ovenproof ramekins and place them in the hot water in the roasting tin. Bake in the oven for 30 minutes until firm. Remove from the tin and allow to cool.

5 Preheat the grill to its highest setting. Replace the water in the roasting tin with 3cm/1¼in cold water and place the ramekins in it. Sprinkle the sugar for the caramel over the custards. Place the tin under the grill, as close as possible to the heat source, for about 5–7 minutes, or until the sugar has caramelized. Leave to cool completely. Serve.

Step 2

Step 3

Step 4

Preparation **20** Min Cooking **35** Min
Per Serving: 373 kcal/1544 kJ;
5g protein; 33g fat; 15g carbohydrate

TYPICALLY PARISIAN
Parisian eateries are known for their luscious desserts and pastries, such as Gâteau Paris-Brest, a praline-filled pastry, and tarts such as Tarte aux Pommes, made with dessert apples. Vanilla Crème Brûlée, another speciality, is sometimes flavoured with fruit and liqueurs.

COOKING TIP

Caramel, or burnt sugar, is often used to add colour or
a crunchy texture to a variety of sweet and savoury
dishes. The golden top for crème brûlée can also be
achieved by melting the sugar in a pan over a
medium heat for 5 minutes, then thinly pouring the
golden liquid over the custards. Leave to harden.

SERVING TIP

Serve these individual crème
brûlées to end a sumptuous
meal of mushroom vol-au-vents,
followed by chicken with asparagus. A small glass
of sweet dessert wine, such as Sauternes, would
round off the meal perfectly.

*M*ARBLED FRUIT FOOL

NORTHERN FRANCE

This is a lighter-than-air dessert of fluffy vanilla cream and smooth strawberry purée folded together to give an elegant marbled effect — the result looks stunning and tastes delicious.

INGREDIENTS
(Serves 6)

- 25g/1oz cornflour
- 250ml/9fl oz milk
- 1 vanilla pod
- 200ml/7fl oz double cream
- 125ml/4fl oz crème fraîche
- 75g/3oz icing sugar
- 275g/10oz strawberries

TO DECORATE

- 142ml/5fl oz whipping cream
- a few strawberries, quartered
- a few mint sprigs

INGREDIENTS TIP

Instead of crème fraîche, mascarpone cheese could be substituted. This will combine with the double cream to make a thick mixture when whisked and will add a tangy flavour to offset the richness of the creamy dessert.

1 In a pan, mix the cornflour with a little milk, then stir in the rest. Slit open the vanilla pod and scrape out the seeds into the pan. Add the vanilla pod to the pan and bring to the boil. Remove from the heat.

2 Whip together the cream and crème fraîche. Sift in 50g/2oz icing sugar and continue whisking until thick. Remove the vanilla pod from the milk, then stir the milk into the creamy mixture.

Step 2

3 Pull the stalks from the strawberries, wash the berries and pat dry. Purée in a food processor or push through a fine sieve. Sift in the remaining icing sugar.

Step 3

4 Transfer the purée to a bowl and add half the vanilla cream. Fold lightly together with a metal spoon, then fold in the rest of the cream. Spoon into 6 serving bowls, cover and chill for 3 hours until firm.

5 Whip the cream and place in a piping bag with a small star nozzle. Remove the mousse from the fridge about 15 minutes before serving to allow it to come to room temperature. Pipe the cream on top and decorate with strawberries and mint sprigs.

Step 4

Preparation **45** Min Chilling **3** Hours
Per Serving: 518 kcal/2147 kJ;
4g protein; 45g fat; 27g carbohydrate

TYPICALLY FRENCH
Brittany, the most westerly area of France, is famous for its deliciously aromatic strawberries. In May and June, the regional markets are full of both wild and cultivated fruit that are made into tarts and gateaux and piled into meringue baskets with cream.

COOKING TIP

When using cornflour to thicken a substance, in this case the vanilla milk, always mix it with a small amount of cold liquid from the recipe before adding it to the main quantity. This avoids unwanted lumps and ensures an excellent, smooth texture.

SERVING TIP

Serve a light, yet sophisticated, main course such as sole in white wine and parsley sauce with French bread and green beans, before rounding off the meal with this colourful whip.

CREAMY YOGHURT WITH BLACKCURRANT SAUCE

THE NETHERLANDS

Orange juice and rind flavour this creamy, yoghurt dessert, which is served with a rich sauce of blackcurrants and crème de cassis. It is unbeatably fruity!

INGREDIENTS

(Serves 4)

FOR THE YOGHURT

- 4 sheets leaf gelatine
- 1 orange
- 200g/7oz natural yoghurt
- 25g/1oz icing sugar
- 25g/1oz caster sugar
- ½ tsp vanilla essence
- 2 egg whites or 1 packet powdered egg white, reconstituted (see page 62)
- 90ml/3fl oz whipping cream

FOR THE SAUCE

- 250g/9oz blackcurrants
- 1 tbsp icing sugar
- 2 tbsp crème de cassis

TO DECORATE

- blackcurrant sprigs
- lemon balm or mint sprigs

INGREDIENTS TIP

Lemon balm is a herb from the mint family. It has a tangy aroma and is good for adding colourful decoration.

1 Soak the gelatine in plenty of cold water for 5 minutes. Wash and dry the orange. Finely grate the rind, then cut the orange in half and squeeze the juice.

2 Put the yoghurt, icing sugar, caster sugar, vanilla essence and orange rind into a bowl. Whisk until smooth. Squeeze the water out of the gelatine. Warm the orange juice in a pan, remove from the heat. Add the gelatine and stir until dissolved. Fold into the yoghurt mixture a little at a time.

3 Whisk the egg whites and the cream, in separate bowls, until soft peaks form. Fold the cream, then the egg whites, into the yoghurt. Pour into a 25x15cm/10x6in dish and chill for at least 2–3 hours until set.

4 Wash the blackcurrants and separate from the stalks with a fork. Push through a sieve into a small bowl, stir in the icing sugar and crème de cassis. Chill for 2 hours.

5 Run a warmed knife around the sides of the dessert and turn out. Cut into four with a knife. Put each serving on a plate and drizzle with the sauce. Decorate with blackcurrant and herb sprigs.

Step 1

Step 4

Step 5

Preparation **30** Min
Chilling **2-3** Hours
Per Portion: 251 kcal/1052 kJ;
5g protein; 11g fat; 31g carbohydrate

TYPICALLY DUTCH

Dairy produce plays a very important part in Holland's economy and the flat, fertile Dutch countryside is perfect grazing land for cattle. Cheeses, notably Gouda and Edam, and fine quality butter, yoghurt and cream are all made from the rich milk the cows produce.

COOKING TIP

English blackcurrants only have a short summer season, July to August, but freeze well for up to 6 months. They can also be bought frozen from most supermarkets. To defrost, spread out the blackcurrants on 2 layers of kitchen paper and leave on a baking tray to catch any juice.

SERVING TIP

For a real indulgence, follow this dessert with iced coffee and fancy biscuits. To make the coffee, chill black coffee in the fridge for 2 hours and serve in tall glasses with a scoop of ice cream, topped with whipped cream.

$\mathscr{S}$TRAWBERRY DELIGHT

GREAT BRITAIN

INGREDIENTS
(Serves 6)

- 4 sheets leaf gelatine
- 100g/4oz white chocolate
- 200ml/7fl oz milk
- 1 lemon
- 250g/9oz strawberries
- 25g/1oz caster sugar
- ½ tsp vanilla essence
- 200ml/7fl oz whipping cream

TO DECORATE
- 125ml/4fl oz whipping cream
- 25g/1oz caster sugar
- ½ tsp vanilla essence
- a few strawberries, sliced

INGREDIENTS TIP

Vanilla sugar can be used instead of the caster sugar and vanilla essence. To make it see page 63.

Melted white chocolate is mixed with a sweetened strawberry purée and whipped cream. Serve this with swirls of cream and sliced strawberries for a typically British dessert.

1 Soak the gelatine in a small bowl with plenty of cold water for 5 minutes. Break up the chocolate. Put into a bowl with the milk and place over a pan of simmering water. Stir gently until melted. Leave to cool.

2 Wash the lemon in hot water, pat dry and grate half the peel. Squeeze the juice from one half. Wash the strawberries, pat dry and remove the stalks. Purée the fruit in a blender with the sugar and vanilla essence. Transfer to a bowl, then stir in the peel and juice.

3 Transfer the chocolate milk to a bowl. Squeeze the excess water from the gelatine. Dissolve it in 3 tablespoons of water in a cup standing in a pan of hot water. Add to the chocolate milk. Stir in the strawberry purée. Whip the cream until thick, then fold into the mixture. Rinse out a 1.2 litre/2 pint long jelly mould with cold water and spoon in the mixture. Chill for 3 hours until set.

4 Dip the mould into very hot water for 15 seconds to release the mousse, then turn out onto a serving plate. Whip the cream; stir in the sugar and vanilla essence. Pipe with cream and decorate with strawberry slices.

Step 2

Step 4

Step 4

Preparation **30** Min Chilling **3** Hours
Per Serving: 365 kcal/1517 kJ;
4g protein; 29g fat; 23g carbohydrate

TYPICALLY BRITISH
Strawberries grow in the flat East Anglian countryside around Cambridge and are ready to be picked in June. At this time of year the Cambridge University students have finished their exams so can enjoy the warm days picnicking and punting on the river Cam.

COOKING TIP

The dessert can be made in any mould with a capacity of 1.2 litre/2 pints but avoid one that is very wide or the turned out dessert will collapse. To check a mould's capacity, fill a measuring jug with water to the required level and pour it into the mould. The liquid should fill the mould without overflowing.

SERVING TIP

To add an exotic touch to your dessert, serve with a kiwi purée. Peel the kiwi fruit, sieve the flesh into a bowl to remove the seeds and sweeten to taste if necessary.

RASPBERRY SHORTCAKE

Rich, buttery shortbread is topped with whipped cream and vibrant fresh raspberries, then decorated with more shortbread wedges for a dramatic summer dessert.

INGREDIENTS

(Serves 4)

FOR THE SHORTBREAD

- 225g/8oz butter
- 150g/5oz caster sugar
- 275g/10oz plain flour
- 100g/4oz ground rice

FILLING AND DECORATION

- 450g/1lb raspberries or tayberries
- 142ml/5fl oz double cream
- 1 tbsp icing sugar, plus extra to dust
- mint sprigs

INGREDIENTS TIP

Ground rice is creamy-white, with a grainy texture, similar to semolina. It is added to biscuit doughs — particularly shortbread — to give a fine, crisp texture. It can also be used in milk puddings or to thicken sauces. It is available from large supermarkets.

1 Preheat the oven to 190°C/375°F/Gas 5. Grease two loose-bottomed, 23cm/9in sandwich tins. Beat the butter with the sugar until creamy. Sieve in the flour and ground rice and press the mixture together with your fingers to make a soft, smooth dough.

2 Press two-thirds of the dough into the base of one tin. Press the remainder into the second. Flute the edge with the prongs of a fork and mark eight wedges with the back of a knife. Prick both dough rounds with a fork. Bake the thicker one for 40–50 minutes, and the thinner one for 30 minutes, until golden.

Step 2

3 Re-mark the thinner wedges. Remove each round from its tin and leave to cool on a rack. Cut the thinner round into wedges. Rinse the raspberries or tayberries and pat dry on kitchen paper. Whip the cream with the icing sugar until soft peaks form.

Step 3

4 Place the thicker round on a plate and spread with the cream. Cover with most of the berries, then stand the shortbread wedges at angles, slightly overlapping, on top. Arrange the remaining berries in the centre, dust with icing sugar and decorate with the mint sprigs.

Step 4

Preparation **25** Min Cooking **50** Min
Per Serving: 614 kcal/2564 kJ;
6g protein; 37g fat; 69g carbohydrate

TYPICALLY SCOTTISH

The Tayside region of Scotland is well known for its tayberries. These large, bright purple berries have a long, conical shape and are a blackberry and raspberry hybrid. Developed in Scotland, they have the aroma and flavour of ripe blackberries.

COOKING TIP

Using loose-bottomed sandwich tins makes the shortbread rounds even in shape and size, and easy to remove after baking. However, if you do not have two loose-bottomed tins, gently press each piece of dough to the required shape on a large baking tray using the flat of your hand or a rolling pin.

SERVING TIP

Serve this dessert after a main course of grilled king prawns. Accompany the meal with a chilled medium-sweet white wine, such as a German Muller-Thurgau or Riesling.

MERINGUE TOWERS WITH MIXED BERRIES

GREAT BRITAIN

Meringues always look spectacular and taste delicious, yet are deceptively easy to make. Here, their sweetness is balanced by the light citrus filling and decoration of tart juicy berries.

INGREDIENTS
(Serves 4)

- 2 egg whites or 1 sachet powdered egg white, reconstituted (see page 62)
- 100g/4oz icing sugar
- 2 tbsp lemon marmalade
- 4 tbsp cream cheese
- 90ml/3fl oz whipping cream
- 1 tbsp caster sugar
- 2 drops vanilla essence
- 75g/3oz raspberries
- 75g/3oz blackberries

TO DECORATE
- lemon balm or mint leaves
- icing sugar

INGREDIENTS TIP

You can use orange marmalade instead of lemon, or your favourite jam. Other mixed berry combinations, such as blueberries and raspberries also work well.

1 Preheat the oven to 110°C/225°F/Gas ¼. Whisk the egg whites with the icing sugar in a heatproof bowl over a pan of simmering water for about 5 minutes or until soft peaks form. Remove the bowl from the heat and leave the meringue to cool. Whisk again for about 3 minutes or until stiff.

Step 1

2 Draw 8 circles, 9cm/3½in diameter, on a sheet of non-stick baking paper. Turn the baking paper marked-side down onto a baking tray. Spoon the meringue into a piping bag fitted with a small plain nozzle.

3 Pipe a flat spiral of meringue over each circle, working from the centre outwards. Bake the meringues for 1½ hours until crisp. Remove from the oven and leave to cool.

Step 3

4 Stir the marmalade into the cream cheese until blended. In another bowl, whisk the cream until soft peaks form, then beat in the sugar and vanilla. Wash and dry the berries.

5 Spoon the cheese mixture onto 4 of the meringues and cover each with a second meringue. Top with the whipped cream and berries. Decorate with lemon balm or mint leaves and dust with icing sugar.

Step 5

Preparation **40** Min
Cooking **1** Hour **30** Min
Per Serving: 261 kcal/1092 kJ;
3g protein; 13g fat; 35g carbohydrate

TYPICALLY BRITISH

Windsor Castle was built for Henry III in the 11th century and later added to by Elizabeth I At its heart is the round tower of which the meringues are a miniature. It is the largest inhabited castle in the world and the favourite home of the Royal family.

COOKING TIPS

Meringues keep fresh in an airtight container for
about one month, but as they are brittle and break
easily, do not pack them tightly • To spoon the
meringue mixture into a piping bag, place the nozzle
end in the neck of a narrow jug and spread the open
end over the lip. This will leave your hands free.

SERVING TIP

A light fruity drink will complement the
delicate flavour of these meringues.
Make a fresh fruit squash from
puréed, sieved fruit, such as
blackcurrants and strawberries. Add
still or sparkling water and sugar to taste.

$\mathscr{A}$PPLE CHARLOTTE RUSSE

RUSSIA

An elegant moulded dessert with crisp sponge fingers, a delicious apple filling, and swirls of whipped cream. Fresh apple slices add the finishing touch.

INGREDIENTS
(Serves 8)

- 1 lemon
- 700g/1½lb cooking apples
- 1 tsp ground mixed spice
- 2 tbsp clear honey
- 4 sheets leaf gelatine
- 142ml/5fl oz orange juice
- 250g/9oz curd cheese
- 284ml/10fl oz whipping cream
- 2 tbsp apricot jam
- 200g/7oz sponge fingers
- 2 egg whites or 1 sachet powdered egg white, reconstituted (see page 62)

TO DECORATE

- 142ml/5fl oz whipping cream
- 1 small red eating apple
- 1 tbsp lemon juice

1 Wash and dry the lemon. Grate the rind finely and squeeze the juice. Peel, core and slice the apples. Simmer the apple slices, lemon rind and juice in a pan for 10 minutes, stirring occasionally, until soft. Add the spice and honey. Cook to a purée, then cool.

Step 1

2 Soak the gelatine in plenty of cold water for 5 minutes, then squeeze out. Pour the orange juice into a heatproof bowl. Stand in a pan of simmering water, add the gelatine, stir briskly to dissolve. Remove from the heat.

Step 2

3 Beat the curd cheese into the apple purée; stir in the orange juice mixture. Whip the cream until stiff and fold into the mixture.

4 Sieve the jam, stir in a few drops of boiling water. Brush the jam onto the sugared side of the sponge fingers and use to line the side of a 20cm/8in loose-bottomed tin, jam sides facing in. Whisk egg whites until stiff, fold into the cheese mixture. Pour into the tin, chill for 3–4 hours or overnight until set.

Step 3

5 Whip the cream until stiff. Core and slice the apple, then sprinkle with lemon juice. Carefully slide the dessert onto a plate. Decorate with the cream and apple slices.

Preparation **1** Hour
Chilling **3–4** Hours
Per Serving: 505 kcal/2157 kJ;
10g protein; 33g fat; 45g carbohydrate

TYPICALLY RUSSIAN

Charlotte Russe is thought to have been invented during the early 19th century by the great French chef, Careme. It became popular at the Russian Court, hence its name, and since then similar desserts have appeared, all surrounded with sponge fingers.

COOKING TIPS

When lining the tin with the sponge fingers, trim one end with a sharp knife so they are more stable when placed upright • To ease the set dessert out of the tin, first run a knife between the sponge fingers and the tin. Then sit the dessert, in the tin, on a mug and carefully ease the tin side down.

SERVING TIP

Serve the Charlotte with a refreshing glass of apple tea. For 8 glasses, place 4 tea bags, 2 tbsp apple juice, a pinch of cinnamon and sugar to taste in a tea pot. Pour over 900ml/1½ pints boiling water and leave to stand for 4 minutes before pouring.

3 WAYS WITH PROFITEROLES

Crisp choux pastry puffs can be served with all kinds of sweet fillings and make the perfect dinner party or buffet dessert.

BASIC CHOUX PUFFS RECIPE

This is the easiest pastry of all to make and it is light and crisp every time.

(MAKES 20 PUFFS)
- 50g/2oz butter
- pinch of salt
- 100g/4oz strong plain flour
- 3 medium eggs

1 Preheat the oven to 220°C/425°F/Gas 7. Line a tray with non-stick baking paper.

2 Place 125ml/4fl oz water in a pan with the butter, chopped into pieces, and salt and bring to a fast boil. Remove from the heat, add the flour and beat hard until the mixture forms a smooth ball and leaves the side of the pan clean. Leave to cool.

3 Whisk the eggs, then gradually beat into the mixture until smooth. Spoon into a piping bag with a medium-sized star nozzle. Pipe small balls onto the baking tray. Bake for 15 minutes. Remove and cut in half immediately, ready for filling, and leave to cool.

STRAWBERRY PUFFS

Preparation **45** Min   Cooking **15** Min

GERMANY

FOR THE FILLING
- 125g/4½oz strawberries
- 250g/9oz full-fat soft cheese
- 2 tbsp icing sugar
- 2 tbsp orange juice or liqueur
- icing sugar, to dust

4 Wash the berries, remove the stalks, then chop. Stir into the soft cheese with the icing sugar and orange juice or liqueur.

5 Fill the profiteroles with the strawberry cheese mixture and dust with icing sugar.

MINI CHOUX BUNS WITH MIXED BERRIES

Preparation **45** Min Cooking **15** Min

SWEDEN

FOR THE FILLING
- l00g/4oz mixed berries
- 25g/1oz caster sugar
- ½ tsp vanilla essence
- 142ml/5fl oz whipping cream
- 75g/3oz icing sugar
- 2 tbsp lemon juice

5 Whip the cream until soft peaks form, then fold in the berries. Fill the choux puffs with the cream mixture.

6 Mix together the icing sugar and the lemon juice until smooth. Spoon the lemon icing over the tops of the choux puffs.

4 Wash and dry the berries. Mix with the sugar and vanilla essence.

DARK CHOCOLATE PROFITEROLES

Preparation **45** Min Cooking **15** Min

NORTHERN FRANCE

FOR THE FILLING
- 125g/6oz good-quality plain chocolate
- 284ml/10fl oz double cream
- 1 tbsp caster sugar

4 Chop the chocolate into pieces and melt in a heatproof bowl over a pan half full of gently simmering water.

5 Whip the cream and sugar until stiff, then fold in half the melted chocolate. Chill for 30 minutes until thick enough to hold its shape.

6 Spoon or pipe the chocolate cream into the bottom half of each choux puff. Replace each top and drizzle with the rest of the melted chocolate.

EXOTIC MANGO MOUSSE

INDIA

Sweet, creamy desserts are popular throughout Asia. This mousse, delicately flavoured with mango, and served with fresh fruit, makes a refreshing end to any meal.

INGREDIENTS
(Serves 6)

- 3 sheets leaf gelatine
- 2 large ripe mangoes
- 1 tbsp lime juice
- 25g/1oz caster sugar
- pinch of salt
- 200ml/7fl oz whipping cream

TO DECORATE
- 2 ripe mangoes
- 1 kiwi fruit
- 4 tbsp desiccated coconut, toasted

INGREDIENTS TIP

To ensure that the mango flavour makes an impact, choose very ripe fruit or, alternatively, use canned mangoes. To check if a mango is ripe, cradle it in your hand and press gently. The flesh will give if the fruit is ripe.

1 Soak the leaf gelatine in plenty of cold water for about 5 minutes. Meanwhile, peel the 2 large mangoes and cut the flesh away from the stone. Put the flesh in a blender with the lime juice, sugar and salt, then purée until smooth. Pour into a bowl.

2 Squeeze the water out of the gelatine. Put the gelatine and 4 tablespoons warm water in a cup and stand the cup in a bowl of hot water. Stir briskly until the gelatine is completely dissolved. Add to the mango purée a little at a time, stirring constantly.

3 Chill the mango mixture for 30–35 minutes until it starts to set. Whip the cream until soft peaks form and fold into the mixture. Cover and chill for 2 hours until set.

4 Just before serving, peel the remaining mangoes and the kiwi fruit and cut each into long fine slices.

5 Remove the mousse from the fridge and scoop it out with a tablespoon. Arrange three scoops radiating out from the centre of each serving plate and add the fruit slices in between. Sprinkle with the toasted coconut.

Step 1

Step 2

Step 4

Preparation **40** Min
Chilling **2** Hours **35** Min
Per Serving: 291 kcal/1209 kJ;
3g protein; 22g fat; 20g carbohydrate

TYPICALLY INDIAN

Ancient mango groves can be found on the slopes of the Himalayas in northern India. The Indians have been cultivating this vivid, highly aromatic fruit for over 4000 years and mangoes are as commonplace throughout Asia as apples in Europe.

COOKING TIP

To toast the desiccated coconut, heat a dry small pan,
or frying pan, for about 1 minute. Keep the heat on
medium. Add the coconut, and spread it out with a
wooden spoon; stir for 30 seconds to 1 minute until
it is golden brown, but do not allow it to burn.

SERVING TIP

This exotic dessert is the perfect finish
to a meal featuring curried vegetables
— tomatoes, potatoes and chilli in
a creamy coconut sauce. Traditional
lemonade makes a good thirst-quencher.

ℬRAZILIAN BANANA CREAM

A soft, fluffy cloud of puréed banana and whipped cream is subtly flavoured with spices and lime juice. Fanned banana slices and a dusting of drinking chocolate complete the dessert.

INGREDIENTS
(Serves 4)

- 2 limes
- 3 ripe bananas
- 2 tbsp brown sugar
- ½ tsp vanilla essence
- pinch of ground ginger
- pinch of ground cloves
- pinch of ground cinnamon
- 142ml/5fl oz whipping cream

TO DECORATE
- 1 tbsp drinking chocolate

INGREDIENTS TIP
Brown sugar is softer and stickier than white and adds a pleasant caramel flavour to desserts. It is available in light and dark varieties. Light brown sugar is better for this recipe.

1 Wash the limes in hot water and dry with kitchen paper. Grate the rind finely. Squeeze out the juice into a bowl, and reserve 2 tablespoons in a separate bowl.

2 Peel two bananas and purée with a hand-held blender or mash thoroughly with a fork. Immediately stir the sugar, grated lime rind and juice into the banana purée so it does not discolour.

Step 1

3 Add the vanilla essence, ginger, cloves and cinnamon to the banana purée, then stir to mix well. Whip the cream in a bowl until soft peaks form and fold in.

4 Peel the remaining banana, cut in half, then in half lengthways so you have 4 pieces. Slice through each piece several times, without cutting right to the end, and gently fan the slices out. Sprinkle with the reserved lime juice to prevent discolouring.

Step 2

5 Divide the banana cream between four plates and arrange a banana fan next to each. Lightly sprinkle the banana with drinking chocolate and serve immediately.

Step 4

Preparation 20 Min
Per Portion: 301 kcal/1257 kJ;
2g protein; 18g fat; 35g carbohydrate

TYPICALLY BRAZILIAN
Bananas reached Brazil in the 16th century when fruit and plants were transported on Portuguese slave ships from west Africa to Latin America. Many types are grown in Brazil, from the familiar larger fruit to a miniature variety called fingers of gold.

COOKING TIP

Serve decorated with shavings of chocolate rather than a dusting of drinking chocolate. Use a bar of plain chocolate at cool room temperature and either grate or run a potato peeler down the chocolate to shave off tiny curls. If the chocolate is too hard, the shavings will break rather than curl.

SERVING TIP

Serve the banana cream in small dessert dishes; scatter with fine shreds of lime rind. A dessert wine such as Marsala would complement its fruity flavour.

CARIBBEAN PINEAPPLE CLOUD

This exotic pineapple mousse is brimming with Caribbean tropical fruit and rum flavours. It is served with a light vanilla-cream sauce and fresh raspberries.

INGREDIENTS
(Serves 4)

- 400g/14oz can pineapple slices
- 75g/3oz brown sugar
- 2 tbsp cornflour
- 2 tbsp rum
- 2 egg whites or 1 packet powdered egg white, reconstituted (see page 62)
- 25g/1oz unsalted butter
- 75g/3oz icing sugar
- 142ml/5fl oz whipping cream
- 1 tsp vanilla essence
- 75g/3oz raspberries

INGREDIENTS TIP

Instead of canned fruit slices, use a fresh pineapple and pineapple juice. When buying pineapples fresh, follow your nose! Ripe fruit has a sweet, aromatic scent. The small leaves at the crown of the pineapple can be pulled out easily and used for decoration.

1 Drain the pineapple slices, reserving 2 tablespoons of juice and 2 slices for decoration. Purée the fruit with a hand blender or a food processor, then place in a saucepan with the brown sugar.

Step 1

2 In a cup, blend the cornflour with the reserved juice to make a smooth paste, then stir into the puréed fruit. Place the pan over a high heat and stir continuously until the mixture thickens. Leave to cool, then stir in the rum.

3 Whisk the egg whites until soft peaks form. Pour in the pineapple mixture and stir thoroughly with a metal spoon. Cover and chill for 2 hours.

Step 3

4 To make the sauce, melt the butter in a saucepan over a medium heat. Remove from the heat and stir in the icing sugar. Gradually fold in the cream and vanilla essence with a spatula or large metal spoon.

5 Roughly chop the reserved pineapple slices. Divide the mousse between 4 dessert bowls and decorate with the chopped pineapple and raspberries. Serve at once, with the vanilla sauce.

Step 5

Preparation **30** Min Chilling **2** Hours
Per Serving: 314 kcal/1321 kJ;
2g protein; 11g fat; 51g carbohydrate

TYPICALLY CARIBBEAN

The Caribbean island of Martinique is situated in the Windward Islands group of the West Indies. Traditional dishes combine fish, chicken and meat with local ingredients such as pineapples and spices. Desserts are often flavoured with rum.

COOKING TIPS

Melt the butter gently as it burns and browns
very quickly if the heat is too intense • Chop the
pineapple slices roughly before putting in the
food processor or using a hand-held blender — the
pieces will fit around the blades better and therefore
purée more quickly.

SERVING TIP

Serve the mousse with a deliciously
creamy cocktail. For 1 drink blend together
50ml/2fl oz each pineapple juice, orange
juice and white rum with 50ml/2fl oz
coconut cream. Decorate the glass with a
slice of pineapple.

SERVING TIP For a variation on this delicious dessert, cut a banana into chunks and layer in a tall glass with scoops of the ice cream. Top with a swirl of whipped cream and a chocolate flake.

TROPICAL COCONUT ICE CREAM

BARBADOS

Give your guests a taste of the Caribbean with this easy-to-make coconut ice cream. The lime syrup adds a lovely tangy topping to a perfect prepare-ahead dessert.

INGREDIENTS
(Serves 6)

- 1 vanilla pod
- 200ml/7fl oz whipping cream
- 50g/2oz caster sugar
- pinch of salt
- 300ml/½ pint canned coconut milk
- 125ml/4fl oz double cream

FOR THE SYRUP
- 3 limes
- 100g/4oz caster sugar

TO DECORATE
- 125ml/4fl oz whipping cream

INGREDIENTS TIP
Coconut milk can be bought canned in most large supermarkets. Shake the can before opening as the milk and solids tend to separate. Creamed coconut can be diluted with boiling water to make coconut milk.

1 Slice open the vanilla pod lengthways and scrape out the seeds. Put the seeds, pod, whipping cream, sugar and salt into a pan. Warm gently over a low heat, stirring with a wooden spoon, until the sugar has melted. Remove from the heat, stir in the coconut milk and leave to cool.

2 Remove the vanilla pod from the pan and stir in the double cream. Pour into a 1.2 litre/2 pint freezer container, cover and freeze for at least 6 hours until frozen solid.

3 Wash the limes in hot water and pat dry with kitchen paper. Remove the rind in thin strips with a canelle knife or peel finely with a knife and cut into strips. Cut the limes in half and squeeze the juice.

4 Put the lime juice, sugar, most of the rind and 250ml/9fl oz water in a small pan. Bring to the boil and simmer for 10 minutes until syrupy. Remove from the heat. Cool.

5 Transfer the ice cream to the fridge 1 hour before serving. Whip the cream into soft peaks. Scoop the ice cream into serving bowls. Pipe on cream swirls, pour over the lime syrup and decorate with remaining lime strips.

Step 1

Step 3

Step 4

Preparation **30** Min Freezing **6** Hours
Defrosting **30** Min
Per Serving: 555 kcal/2306 kJ;
2g protein; 44g fat; 40g carbohydrate

TYPICALLY BARBADIAN
European colonies grew lime crops on the island for the first time in the early 16th century. Today we think of limes as being essentially Caribbean. They are used to add a citrus tang to many dishes, as well as cocktails such as fruity rum punches and daiquiris.

CHERRY PAVLOVA

AUSTRALIA

This crisp meringue has a deliciously soft, chewy centre. Piled high with mini meringues, whipped cream and jewel-like cherries, it's a star performer every time.

INGREDIENTS

(Serves 8)

FOR THE MERINGUE
- 3 egg whites
- pinch of salt
- 175g/6oz caster sugar
- 1 tsp white wine vinegar
- 1 tbsp cornflour

FOR THE FILLING
- 680g/1lb 7oz jar Morello cherries
- 250ml/9fl oz whipping cream
- 25g/1oz caster sugar

INGREDIENTS TIP

Use fresh cherries for this recipe when in season, or, as these can be expensive, try another fresh fruit such as raspberries.

1 Preheat the oven to 130°C/250°F/Gas ½. Beat the egg whites and salt with an electric whisk for about 5 minutes, or until soft peaks form. Whisk in half the sugar, a tablespoon at a time, beating well after each addition to dissolve the sugar. Carefully fold in the remaining sugar with the vinegar and cornflour using a large metal spoon.

Step 2

2 Draw an 18cm/7in circle on a sheet of non-stick baking paper. Turn it face down on a baking sheet. Spoon the meringue into a piping bag with a large star nozzle. Pipe just over half the mixture in a flat spiral to fill the circle, starting at the outside and working in. Pipe a second layer over the outer ring to make it thicker than the rest.

Step 3

3 Pipe the remaining meringue into small rosettes at one end of the paper. Bake for 1 hour, or until crisp. Turn the oven off and leave the meringues to cool in the oven.

4 Rinse the cherries in cold water. Drain, then remove any stones. Whip the cream and sugar together until stiff and spoon into the meringue base. Arrange the cherries and meringue rosettes on the top.

Step 4

Preparation 45 Min Cooking 2 Hours
Per Serving: 283 kcal/1183 kJ;
2g protein; 15g fat; 36g carbohydrate

TYPICALLY AUSTRALIAN
Australians claim Pavlova as their own, maintaining it was created in 1935 by a hotel chef in Perth who made it in honour of the visiting Russian ballerina, Anna Pavlova, having been inspired by the floating white cloud of her ballet skirt.

COOKING TIPS

Pavlova is baked at a slightly higher oven temperature than ordinary meringue so only the outside becomes crisp and the centre stays soft and chewy • Add the fruit and cream filling no more than 1 hour before serving so the meringue does not soften too much.

SERVING TIP

Lightly toasted almonds sprinkled over the top will balance the sweetness of the meringue. An ideal main course to serve before this dessert would be grilled lamb chops and mixed vegetables.

CALIFORNIAN CHEESECAKE

USA

A crisp, biscuity base is spiced with aromatic cinnamon and topped with a deliciously smooth mixture of soft cheese and golden peaches in this creamy fruit dessert.

INGREDIENTS
(Serves 8)

- 175g/6oz digestive biscuits
- 2 tbsp caster sugar
- 1 tsp ground cinnamon
- 75g/3oz butter, melted

FOR THE FILLING
- 4 sheets leaf gelatine
- 1 small lemon
- 200g/7oz full-fat cream cheese
- 450g/1lb curd cheese
- 3 tbsp icing sugar
- 800g/1¾lb can peach slices
- 200ml/7fl oz whipping cream

TO DECORATE
- 800g/1¾lb can peach slices
- lemon balm or mint leaves

INGREDIENTS TIP

Peaches canned in juice rather than syrup are less sweet and will make a fruity foil for the creamy filling.

1 Put the biscuits in a plastic bag and break up into fine crumbs by crushing with a rolling pin. Place in a bowl and mix with the sugar, cinnamon and butter. Press over the the base of a 23cm/9in spring-form cake tin. Chill in the fridge for 1 hour.

2 Soak the gelatine in plenty of cold water for 5 minutes. Wash the lemon and dry. Finely grate the rind and squeeze the juice.

3 Beat together the cream cheese, curd cheese, icing sugar, lemon rind and juice. Drain one can of peach slices into a bowl, purée with a hand-held blender, then gradually stir into the cheese mixture.

4 Squeeze the water out of the gelatine and dissolve in 3 tablespoons of warm water in a pan over a low heat. Beat into the cheese mixture. Whip the cream in another bowl until soft peaks form, then fold in.

5 Arrange half the peach slices from the second can on the biscuit base and cover with the cream mixture. Chill for 3 hours, or until set. Serve decorated with the remaining peach slices and lemon balm or mint leaves.

Step 1

Step 3

Step 5

Preparation **40** Min Chilling **4** Hours
Per Portion: 325 kcal/1352 kJ;
5g protein; 23g fat; 25g carbohydrate

TYPICALLY CALIFORNIAN
In the sun-kissed state of California, huge plantations of thousands of peach trees provide fruit for export all over the world. The variety of peach cultivated there is also excellent for preserving and a large part of the crop is canned.

COOKING TIP

Roughly break up the biscuits first before crushing them in the plastic bag. If you prefer to use a food processor, add the biscuits down the feeder tube one at a time with the motor running so they crush evenly and lumps of biscuit do not clog the blade.

SERVING TIP

Serve with iced coffee. To make this, chill coffee, with or without milk and sugar, for 2 hours. Serve in tall glasses topped with a scoop of vanilla ice cream or with piped whipped cream.

SERVING TIP Although excellent on its own, the soufflé could be served with fresh orange segments. As an after-dinner drink, indulge in a malt whisky, a bourbon or Drambuie (whisky liqueur) on the rocks.

CHOCOLATE SOUFFLE WITH WHISKEY

USA

Here is a chocolate dessert at its very best. Dark chocolate and smoky whiskey lend their distinctive flavours to this smooth soufflé from the southern state of Tennessee.

INGREDIENTS
(Serves 8)

- 250g/9oz plain chocolate
- 3 sheets leaf gelatine
- 2 tbsp milk
- 90ml/3fl oz whiskey
- 450ml/¾ pint whipping cream
- 4 egg whites or 2 sachets powdered egg white, reconstituted (see page 62)
- 2 tbsp caster sugar

TO DECORATE
- white chocolate shavings

INGREDIENTS TIP

To ensure this soufflé has a rich chocolate flavour, buy fine quality dark chocolate with a high proportion of cocoa solids — 70% is the best if you can find it, but any dark chocolate with over 60% would be suitable.

1 Using a wide-bladed potato peeler, shave off about 50g/2oz of the chocolate and set aside. Break up the rest and melt in a heatproof bowl over a pan half-full of simmering water, then remove from the heat.

Step 1

2 Soak the gelatine in plenty of cold water for 5 minutes. Squeeze the excess water out of the gelatine. Pour the milk into a bowl placed over a pan of hot water and heat gently. Add the gelatine and stir until dissolved. Gradually stir into the chocolate.

3 Stir the whiskey into the cream and whip until soft peaks form. Fold into the chocolate mixture. With a clean whisk, beat the egg whites until peaks form, then whisk in the sugar. Fold into the chocolate mixture.

Step 3

4 Fold a long strip of foil in half, then place it around a 600ml/1 pint soufflé dish, so it stands 5cm/2in above the dish. Secure in place with sticky tape, then pour in the mixture and chill for 3 hours.

5 Remove the foil. Press the white chocolate shavings around the edge of the soufflé using a palette knife. Sprinkle the reserved plain chocolate shavings over the top.

Step 5

Preparation **50** Min Chilling **3** Hours
Per Serving: 352 kcal/1462 kJ;
g protein; 27g fat; 19g carbohydrate

TYPICALLY TENNESSEE
Rye whiskey has been distilled in Lynchburg, Tennessee since 1866. Made from grain with a high maize content, it has a bitter flavour and is highly regarded among whiskey connoisseurs. It can be used in cooking too, in both sweet and savoury dishes.

RASPBERRY BAKED ALASKA

USA

A light sponge base covered with ice cream and raspberries is topped with meringue, then baked in the oven for an exquisite melt-in-the-mouth hot and cold dessert.

INGREDIENTS
(Serves 4)

FOR THE BASE
- 2 large eggs
- 50g/2oz caster sugar
- 50g/2oz plain flour
- ½ tsp baking powder
- 50g/2oz raspberries

FOR THE MERINGUE
- 2 egg whites
- pinch of salt
- 100g/4oz caster sugar

FOR THE FILLING
- 200ml/7fl oz vanilla ice cream
- 100g/4oz raspberries

TO DECORATE
- 100g/4oz raspberries
- 50g/2oz blackberries

1 Preheat the oven to 180°C/350°F/Gas 4. Grease a 20cm/8in spring-form cake tin. Whisk the eggs and sugar with an electric whisk until very thick and pale. Sift the flour and baking powder. Fold into the mixture.

2 Gently pour into the cake tin. Arrange 50g/2oz raspberries evenly over the top. Bake in the oven for 15–20 minutes until the sponge is golden. Remove from the tin and leave to cool on a wire rack.

3 Increase the oven temperature to 200°C/400°F/Gas 6. Whisk the egg whites 10 minutes before serving, with a pinch of salt until soft peaks form. Gradually add the sugar, a tablespoon at a time, and continue whisking until the mixture is firm and glossy.

4 Put the sponge on a baking sheet covered with foil. For the filling, pile scoops of ice cream on the sponge base and top with raspberries. Spread the meringue over the top and side to cover completely. Pull into peaks with a flat-bladed knife or spatula.

5 Bake in the oven for 7 minutes, or until the meringue has turned golden brown. Serve with raspberries and blackberries.

Step 3

Step 4

Step 4

Preparation **30** Min Cooking **30** Min
Per Portion: 359 kcal/1521 kJ;
9g protein; 9g fat; 65g carbohydrate

TYPICALLY AMERICAN
The soft meringue peaks that adorn this dessert resemble icebergs, hence its association with snowy Alaska. This dish is particularly popular in Oregon where local soft fruits, such as blueberries, are used to give an extra refreshing piquancy.

COOKING TIP

The sponge base needs to be completely cold before the filling and meringue can be added. You can make the sponge the day before and store it in the fridge wrapped in cling film. Or, make the sponge up to 1 month in advance, allow to cool, wrap in freezer film and freeze in a rigid container. Thaw before using.

SERVING TIP

Instead of surrounding the dessert with berries, serve it with a soft fruit compôte made from a mixture of blackberries, raspberries, blueberries or strawberries, sprinkled with sugar and left for 2-3 hours to draw out the fruit juices.

DOUBLE CHOCOLATE MOUSSE

USA

This dark and white chocolate mousse is set in two exquisitely creamy layers. Port flavours the dark mousse, while the white is spiked with sweet orange liqueur.

INGREDIENTS
(Serves 8)

FOR THE DARK MOUSSE
- 100g/4oz plain chocolate
- 142ml/5fl oz whipping cream
- 4 tbsp caster sugar
- 2 tbsp port
- 2 egg whites or 1 sachet powdered egg white, reconstituted (see page 62)

FOR THE WHITE MOUSSE
- 100g/4oz white chocolate
- 125ml/4fl oz whipping cream
- 2 tbsp caster sugar
- 2 tbsp orange liqueur
- 2 egg whites or 1 sachet powdered egg white, reconstituted (see page 62)

TO DECORATE
- chocolate leaves
- 2 tbsp drinking chocolate

1 Chop the plain chocolate and place in a heatproof bowl. Add 3 tablespoons of cream and the caster sugar. Melt slowly over a pan half filled with simmering water. Stir in the port and remove from the heat.

Step 1

2 Whisk the egg whites and the rest of the cream in separate bowls until soft peaks form and fold both into the chocolate mixture. Line an 18cm/7in spring-form cake tin with cling film. Spoon in the chocolate mixture and chill for 2 hours until set.

Step 2

3 To make the white mousse, chop the chocolate and melt with 3 tablespoons of the cream and the sugar in a heatproof bowl over a pan half filled with simmering water. Stir in the liqueur, then remove from the heat.

4 Whisk the egg whites and the rest of the cream in separate bowls until soft peaks form. Fold both into the white chocolate mixture and spread over the dark mousse in the dish. Chill for a further 2 hours until set.

Step 4

5 Loosen the edge of the mousse with a spatula, unclip the tin, then transfer the dessert to a plate. Decorate with chocolate leaves and dust with drinking chocolate.

Preparation **40** Min Chilling **4** Hours
Per Serving: 375 kcal/1561 kJ;
4g protein; 26g fat; 31g carbohydrate

TYPICALLY AMERICAN

New York is America at its most cosmopolitan and its many restaurants serve food and drink around the clock. Late night revellers will often call into a coffee shop or deli for a reviving hot chocolate and a brownie or a cappuccino sprinkled with chocolate.

COOKING TIP

You can buy ready-made chocolate leaves to decorate the mousse or make your own. To make, melt 75g/3oz plain chocolate and, with a small brush, paint the chocolate over the underside of 8 clean, dry bay or rose leaves. Leave to set, then carefully peel the real leaf away from the chocolate one.

SERVING TIP

Instead of leaves, decorate the mousse with small truffles or other chocolates. Finish off with a sprinkling of dark chocolate finely grated over the top of the mousse.

DICTIONARY OF TERMS

Few people can resist a creamy dessert, so make the most of these delicious recipes with this A–Z of terms, techniques, special ingredients and essential kitchen equipment.

Coffee gives a real kick to creamy desserts. Use instant granules for a strong mixture with a concentrated flavour.

Eggs which are either raw or lightly cooked, should not be eaten by infants, pregnant women, the elderly or anyone in poor health. Powdered egg white is pasteurized and is safe in desserts; it is available in sachets from most supermarkets (one sachet is equivalent to two fresh egg whites). Follow the instructions on the sachet for reconstituting the dried egg white with water, then use as directed in the recipe.

Gelatine is a setting agent that comes in either leaf or powder form. Both leaf and powdered are interchangeable in the recipes — use 4 sheets leaf or 1 sachet of powdered gelatine to set 600ml/1 pint of mixture. Soak leaf gelatine in cold water for 5 minutes to soften it. Squeeze out the excess water, then add the leaves to warm liquid from the recipe and stir to dissolve without lumps forming. A vegetarian substitute is also available at most supermarkets. Follow the packet instructions as strengths of setting vary.

Ice cream desserts can be frozen in a freezer at its coldest setting. An ice cream maker can also be used — transfer to a freezer container once the ice cream churn is finished.

Mascarpone is a full-fat soft Italian cheese with a soft buttery consistency making it a favourite ingredient for cooking or serving with desserts.

Meringue is a mixture of stiffly beaten egg whites and sugar, or sometimes a sugar syrup. The sugar is slowly whisked into the egg whites until soft peaks form. The mixture is then baked in the oven until completely dry or just until crisp on the outside and chewy inside.

ALL ABOUT CHOCOLATE

DIFFERENT TYPES
Chocolate with a low cocoa content tastes subtle and sweet, while chocolate with a high

cocoa content tastes sharp and bitter. Added ingredients such as coffee or nuts can affect the sweetness of the chocolate. White chocolate does not contain any cocoa, but has at least 20% cocoa butter in it. It is not as firm as plain chocolate and is much sweeter. Plain chocolate is good for coating, topping and decorating desserts. It has a higher cocoa butter content,

melts more easily and flows better. Milk chocolate has a mild, sweet flavour but is not really strong enough for cooked dishes.

DECORATIVE EFFECTS
To make chocolate leaves; melt chocolate, then paint onto the undersides of bay or rose leaves. Peel away the leaves when the chocolate has set. For shapes, pipe melted chocolate on to foil and leave to set. Use a potato peeler to make chocolate curls.

MELTING CHOCOLATE
Break up chocolate and melt in a heatproof bowl over a pan half full of simmering water; stir the chocolate when it starts to melt. The bowl must be above the water or the chocolate will become grainy.

Mousse is a French term meaning froth or foam. It's also a rich, airy dessert of whisked egg white and cream folded into an egg custard or fruit purée. It can be sweet or savoury, hot or cold.

Sponge fingers are sweet sponge biscuits used in desserts. They are ideal for soaking up alcohol or coffee which are often used as flavourings.

Sugar, especially caster and icing sugar, is often used for soft, creamy desserts. Unrefined brown sugar is only used in the more exotic desserts. Store sugar in an airtight container in a dry place, or the granules will stick together.

Vanilla essence is extracted from vanilla pods. It's used for flavouring on its own or to bring out the flavour of coffee and chocolate. Only use a few drops at a time.

Vanilla pods are the dried seed cases of the orchid plant. They have a very strong aroma and should be used quite sparingly.

Vanilla sugar is deliciously fragrant. It's made by leaving a vanilla pod in a jar of caster sugar for at least two days. Cover the jar with a lid, shake it now and again. Remove the pod, wash and dry it, and use again. The vanilla sugar, which will be delicately flavoured, can be used as a substitute for sugar and vanilla essence in dessert recipes.

Waxed lemons Some lemons are wax coated to preserve them. Scrub in warm water before use.

Whisking egg white increases its volume by up to eight times, providing a light and airy texture to a dish. Beat with a hand or electric whisk until soft white peaks form. Add a pinch of salt or sugar, or a squeeze of lemon juice and whisk the mixture until stiff peaks form.

INDEX

Acknowledgements

Picture Credits
All cover and recipe pictures:
Meister Verlag/International Masters Publisher B.V.
Michael Brauner, Dorothee Gödert, Ansgar Pudens, Peter Rees,
Manuel Schnell, Karl Adamson
Agency pictures:
Pictures for the Typically Sections: AKG: Page 52; Anzenberger:
T. Anzenberger Page 12, Page 51, Appelt Page 56, Sioen Page 46;
Bilderberg: Boisvieux Page 44, Franke Page 8, Page 26, Grames Page 48,
Horacek Page 28; Focus: Snowdon/Hoyer Page 30; Food Features: Page 18;
F. M. Frei: Page 14; IFA: TPL Page 24; Image Bank: Hartmann Page 21,
Pistolesi Page 60; Kader: Jürgen Page 22; Look: Heeb Page 58, Martini
Page 7; Mauritius: Pascal Page 54, Thonig Page 32, Waldkirch Page 40;
Robert Harding: Page 36, Page 38; Visionbank: Page 34; White Star:
Reichelt Page 16

Measuring Ingredients
Tsp — teaspoon, Tbsp — tablespoon
Teaspoons and tablespoons are level and measured using standard
measuring spoons.
Follow either metric or imperial measurements and don't mix the two.

© International Masters Publishers BV/
International Masters Publishers Ltd MCMXCVIII
Reproduced by Studio One Origination, London, UK
Printed in Verona, Italy, by Druck Mondadori